Eating Green

Molly Aloian

🌳 Crabtree Publishing Company

www.crabtreebooks.com

Author
Molly Aloian

Publishing plan research and development
Reagan Miller

Editors
Rachel Eagen, Crystal Sikkens

Proofreader and indexer
Wendy Scavuzzo

Design
Samara Parent

Photo research
Crystal Sikkens

Production coordinator and prepress technician
Samara Parent

Print coordinator
Margaret Amy Salter

Photographs
Dreamstime: page 5 (bottom)
Thinkstock: cover, pages 5 (top), 6, 12, 15, 17 (bottom)
All other images by Shutterstock

Library and Archives Canada Cataloguing in Publication

Aloian, Molly, author
    Eating green / Molly Aloian.

(The green scene)
Includes index.
Issued in print and electronic formats.
ISBN 978-0-7787-0263-4 (bound).--ISBN 978-0-7787-0277-1
(pbk.).--ISBN 978-1-4271-1267-5 (pdf).--ISBN 978-1-4271-9436-7
(html)

    1. Food--Juvenile literature. 2. Sustainable living--Juvenile
literature. I. Title.

TX355.A55 2013   j641.3   C2013-905207-0
                                      C2013-905208-9

Library of Congress Cataloging-in-Publication Data

Aloian, Molly.
    Eating green / Molly Aloian.
        pages cm. -- (The green scene)
    Includes index.
    ISBN 978-0-7787-0263-4 (reinforced library binding) -- ISBN 978-0-7787-
0277-1 (pbk.) -- ISBN 978-1-4271-1267-5 (electronic pdf) -- ISBN 978-1-4271-
9436-7 (electronic html)
    1. Environmentalism--Juvenile literature. 2. Sustainable agriculture--
Juvenile literature. I. Title.

GE195.5.A46 2013
641.028'6--dc23

                        2013030078

Crabtree Publishing Company

www.crabtreebooks.com   1-800-387-7650

Printed in Canada/092013/BF20130815

Published in Canada
Crabtree Publishing
616 Welland Ave.
St. Catharines, Ontario
L2M 5V6

Published in the United States
Crabtree Publishing
PMB 59051
350 Fifth Avenue, 59th Floor
New York, New York 10118

Published in the United Kingdom
Crabtree Publishing
Maritime House
Basin Road North, Hove
BN41 1WR

Published in Australia
Crabtree Publishing
3 Charles Street
Coburg North
VIC 3058

Contents

Eating away at Earth........................4

Eating green.................................6

Packaging piles up.........................8

Fresh fruits and veggies..........10

Stay away from spray.............12

Learn about local..................14

Drinking green....................16

A litter-free lunch................18

Family mealtime....................20

Pizza time!..............................22

Learning more..........................23

Words to know and Index...........24

Eating away at Earth

What and how we eat can harm the environment. We often throw away huge amounts of food packaging that ends up in **landfills**. Many of the fruits and vegetables we buy have been sprayed with dangerous chemicals that also cause **pollution**.

We often eat take-out meals in a hurry without thinking about how much packaging we will throw away.

4

Food pollution

Most of the foods we eat come from far away. Every day, tons of harmful **fossil fuels** are burned to get these foods to and from grocery stores. Burning fossil fuels causes pollution.

Oranges and other fruits can travel 2,500 miles (4,023 kilometers) or more before they are delivered to grocery stores.

Eating green

Eating green means understanding the **impact** our food choices have on the environment and trying to lessen that impact. To eat green, we must buy food with little or no packaging. We should eat fresh food and local food that is grown or made nearby. Eating green also means avoiding foods that have been sprayed with harmful **pesticides**.

Reduce waste and pollution by *recycling* or *reusing* food cans and other packaging.

Take Action!

Both women in these pictures are buying tomatoes. Which one is eating more green? Why?

FRESH LOCAL PRODUCE

POIDS NET 20 lb
9.08 kg

Packaging piles up

Many of the foods we buy are wrapped in packaging. Some packaging is useful because it stops food from getting squished. Other packaging is there only to make the food look good. For example, granola bars come in a box and each bar is wrapped in plastic. Often, the box and plastic wrappers both end up in landfills.

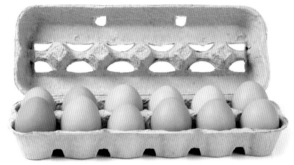

Cardboard egg cartons protect eggs from being broken and can be recycled.

8

In landfills

Tons of food and drink packaging ends up buried in landfills. In fact, each person in the United States sends over 250 pounds (113 kilograms) of packaging to landfills every year. Landfills pollute the land, air, and water.

Fresh fruits and veggies

Fast food and **processed** meats, cheese, and sugary snack foods are bad for the environment and bad for our bodies. These foods are made in huge factories that cause pollution and use a lot of packaging. These foods also contain harmful **preservatives** and other chemicals.

Cookies made in factories are packaged in plastic trays and wrappers, which end up in landfills.

Fresh is best

Eating fresh fruits and vegetables is good for your body and good for the environment. These foods contain important **nutrients** that your body needs to stay healthy. They also cause less pollution than foods from factories.

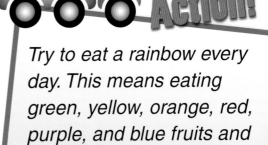

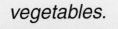

Try to eat a rainbow every day. This means eating green, yellow, orange, red, purple, and blue fruits and vegetables.

Stay away from spray

Many food crops are sprayed with pesticides and other chemicals. Pesticides kill the pests that damage food crops, but they are harmful to people and harmful to the environment. Pesticides cause pollution and they are bad for our health.

The man is wearing a mask to help prevent the harmful spray from getting into his lungs.

Organic foods

Try to avoid foods that have been sprayed with pesticides. Buy **organic** food or grow your own. Organic food is grown in as natural a way as possible. Organic fruits and vegetables are better for the environment and better for your body.

Take Action!

Talk to your parents about growing some of your own fruits and vegetables in a small area of your backyard, in a window box, or in pots.

13

Huge trucks, trains, and airplanes carry many foods long distances. These vehicles burn fossil fuels that pollute the air, land, and water. Burning fossil fuels produces dangerous **greenhouse gases** that remain in Earth's **atmosphere**.

Food in grocery stores is labeled so we know where it comes from. Where does your food come from?

Farm fresh

Local foods are better for the environment because they are grown nearby. Many local foods are also organic. Ask your family to walk or ride bicycles to a local farmers' market a few times a week. You will help reduce pollution and buy healthier food.

Take Action!

A fun exercise you can try with your family is eating only local food for an entire month. Can you do it?

Some stores make an effort to carry local food.

Drinking green

Plastic bottles take hundreds of years to break down.

Nearly 5 billion drink boxes are thrown away each year. Eight out of every ten plastic water bottles end up in landfills. One way to reduce waste is by purchasing drinks in glass containers, which can easily be recycled. Another option is making your own freshly squeezed juice at home!

Remember to recycle

Every year, 13 billion metal cans, including soda cans, are made in North America. Only about one quarter of the metal used to make the cans has been recycled. Always remember to recycle soda cans.

Take Action!

Instead of drinking from drink boxes or plastic water bottles, bring a reusable container to school filled with water or juice.

A litter-free lunch

Each school year, lunches for an average student produce 67 pounds (30 kg) of packaging and waste. This adds millions of pounds of garbage to landfills in the United States alone. Try to pack a lunch that produces NO garbage at all.

A reusable lunch box is a better option than wrapping your lunch in plastic wrap or aluminum foil.

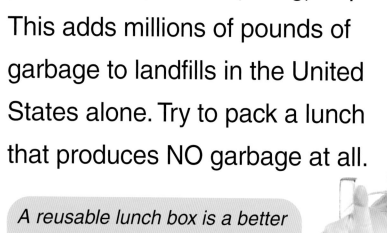

18

Pack green

Avoid plastic bags, plastic yogurt containers, straws, and plastic spoons and forks. Pack your lunch in reusable containers, use metal forks and spoons, and cloth napkins that can be washed and reused.

Take Action!

Did you know that Americans use more than 277 million plastic bags a day? Many of these bags end up in landfills. Cloth bags are a better option because they can be reused over and over again.

Family mealtime

Many people eat in cars or in front of computers or televisions. They often eat too much, too quickly, and do not pay attention to what they are putting into their bodies.

Families often do not talk to each other when they eat their dinner in front of the television.

Food and family

Make a promise to sit down with your family for meals on a regular basis. Talk about where your food came from, how it was grown, and what new foods you would like to try. Eating green is great for the environment and fun for your family!

You can help prepare meals to learn more about the foods you are eating.

Pizza time!

Pizza is a yummy family dinner, but takeout is a poor choice for the environment. Making your own pizza is a fun activity for your family, and it stops a cardboard box from going into a landfill. You will need:

- *A pizza tray and rolling pin*
- *A ball of dough*
- *Pizza sauce*
- *Cheese*
- *Healthy toppings, such as mushroom, onions, tomatoes, and red or green peppers*

1. *Ask an adult to preheat the oven to 425°F (218°C).*
2. *Use a rolling pin to roll out your pizza dough. Carefully move it onto a pizza tray.*
3. *Spread pizza sauce onto the dough.*
4. *Top with grated cheese and any toppings you choose.*
5. *Let it bake for 20–25 minutes. Carefully remove the pizza from the oven with an adult's help, and enjoy!*

Learning more

Books

Apte, Sunita. *Eating Green* (Going Green). Bearport Publishing, 2009.

Bailey, Jacqui. *What's the Point of Being Green?* Franklin Watts, 2011.

Gibbons, Gail. *The Vegetables We Eat*. Holiday House Inc, 2007.

Hardesty, Constance. *Grow Your Own Pizza*. Fulcrum Publishing, 2008.

Websites

Kids Be Green

http://kidsbegreen.org/

How Kids Can Eat Green

www.pbs.org/parents/special/article-earthday-greeneating.html

5 Steps to Sustainable Eating

www.mcgill.ca/fitatmcgill/sustainable/5-steps-sustainable-eating

Sustainable Table

http://www.sustainabletable.org/1117/welcome-to-sustainable-table

Words to know

Note: Some boldfaced words are defined where they appear in the book.

atmosphere (AT-muhs-feer) noun A protective layer of air surrounding Earth

fossil fuels (FOS-uhl FYOO-uhlz) noun Fuels such as oil, natural gas, and coal that are used to power cars, make electricity, and heat and cool homes

greenhouse gases (GREEN-hous GAS-ez) noun Harmful gases that remain trapped in Earth's atmosphere

impact (IM-pakt) noun A strong or forceful effect

landfills (LAND-filz) noun Huge holes in the ground that are filled with garbage and then covered with dirt

local (LOH-kuhl) adjective Close to home

nutrients (NOO-tree-uhnts) noun Natural substances that help living things grow and stay healthy

organic (awr-GAN-ik) adjective Describing food that has been produced or grown naturally

pesticides (PES-tuh-sahydz) noun Chemicals that kill or keep away insects, slugs, mold, weeds, and other pests that damage plants

pollution (puh-LOO-shuhn) noun Chemicals, fumes, waste, or garbage that harm or spoil Earth

preservatives (pri-ZUR-vuh-tivz) noun Chemicals added to food to stop it from spoiling or discoloring

processed (PROS-es-d) adjective Describing something that has been specially treated or prepared to change or preserve it

recycle (ree-SAHY-kuhl) verb To change or process something to be used again, sometimes in a different way

reduce (ri-DOOS) verb To use or produce less

reuse (re-YOOZ) verb To use something again

A noun is a person, place, or thing.
An adjective is a word that tells you what something is like.
A verb is an action word that tells you what someone or something does.

Index

chemicals, 4, 6, 10, 12
drinks, 16, 17
eating fresh, 6, 10, 11
family meals, 20–22
fossil fuels, 5, 14
landfills, 4, 8, 9, 18

local foods, 6, 15
lunches, 18–19
organic foods, 13, 15
packaging, 4, 6, 7, 8, 9, 10
pizza recipe, 22

pollution, 4, 5, 6, 9, 10, 11, 12, 14
processed foods, 10
recycling, 6, 8, 17
reusable items, 6, 17, 19